EN GARDE!

A Girl's Introduction to the World of Fencing

Follow the experiences of a young fencing student and
discover what it is like to be a fencer

Carlos Velez III

Wish Publishing
Terre Haute, Indiana
www.wishpublishing.com

LCCN: 2007939840

Edited by Heather Lowhorn
Editorial assistance provided by Dorothy Chambers
Cover designed by Phil Velikan
Cover by Alexander J. Ripa; Interior photography by Alexander J. Ripa and Carlos Velez III

Printed in the United States of America
10 9 8 7 6 5 4 3 2 1

Published in the United States by
Wish Publishing
P.O. Box 10337
Terre Haute, IN 47801, USA
www.wishpublishing.com

Distributed in the United States by
Cardinal Publishers Group
2222 Hillside Avenue, Suite 100
Indianapolis, Indiana 46218
www.cardinalpub.com

For Dad, because you first taught me the lure of the blade

acknowledgements

Grateful acknowledgement is given to the following schools, clubs, associations, and persons:

Buzzards Bay Fencing Club, Jim Rose, for introducing me to RIFAC;

U.S. Fencing Association;

U.S. Chess Federation;

Rhode Island Fencing Academy and Club, Alexander J. Ripa: Academy's Founder/Head Coach/Photographer and Jill Ripa: Academy's Director/Coach, for their gracious support and expertise, and for their meticulous editing of the manuscript;

And the girls: Renee, McKenzie, Ariel, Caroline, Maddy and Kathryn, for their many thoughtful insights on their training and experiences.

"That's what we need now,
an angel with a flaming sword."
— The Mark of Zorro: 1940

Katie Walker and the fencing team

preface

Fencing is not just a lot of swinging from chandeliers or leaping from balconies. That's just the stuff immortalized by Hollywood movies, all drama and high jinks. Fencing is much, much more. There's something so thrilling when you enter a fencing academy and you hear the tap-tap of blades. It's some kind of magic when you hear it; you know you're entering a whole new world that most people don't know about.

By following the experiences of a young fencing student and discovering what it is like to be a fencer, *En Garde! A Girl's Introduction to the World of Fencing* takes young readers (ages 12-15) through the steps to becoming a beginning fencer. *En Garde!* teaches and illustrates the rules of fencing as well as entertains the reader by bringing her into the world of a 14-year-old fencer.

En Garde! connects the sport of fencing to the intellect of a chess player, the strength of a ballet dancer, the philosophy of a martial arts student, and the cunning of a drama student, while incorporating a short history of fencing with the origins of the duel and weapons.

Fencing is one of the safest competitive sports around. Fencers compete as individuals and in team events, creating a team spirit. But fencing still allows the student to have her own drive. *En Garde!* hopes to inspire the student to really want to fence and to go through the training, which is hard work; it requires both dedication and resilience. You can judge for yourself if fencing is right for you. If so, then *En Garde! A Girl's Introduction to the World of Fencing* is for you.

table of contents

Chapter 1
Courage to Face the Challenge
   Introducing the student...13

Chapter 2
Honor to Be on a Team
   Introducing the fencing academy and club...23

Chapter 3
Choice of Weapon
   Introducing the weapons...39

Chapter 4
Confidence In Yourself
   Introducing the student's home life...53

EN GARDE!

Chapter 5
Commitment To The Sport
    Introducing the future of fencing...65

Chapter 6
Passion For The Game
    Introducing the national tournament...71

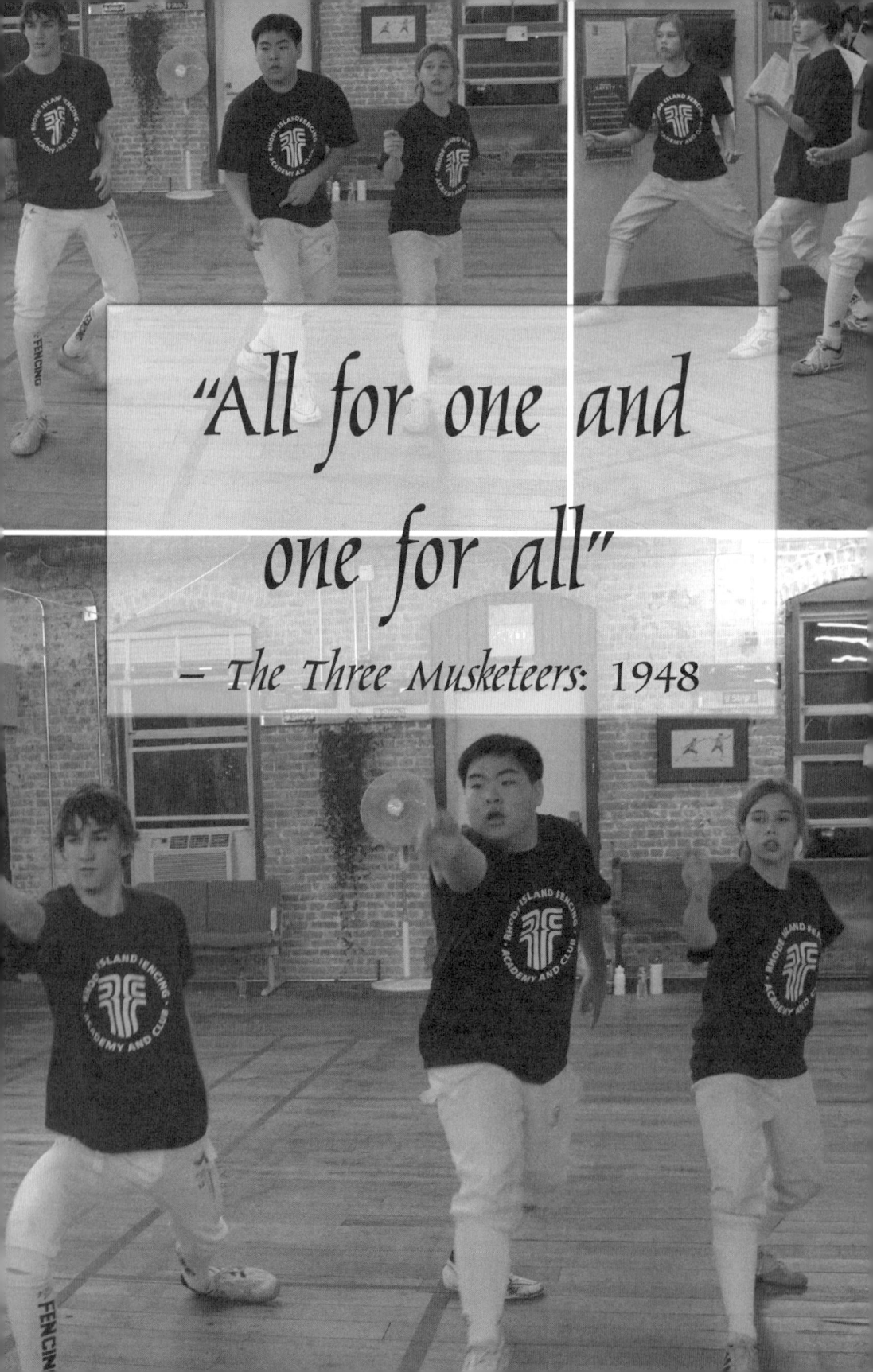

"All for one and one for all"

— The Three Musketeers: 1948

COURAGE

to face the challenge...

"What? You're putting up fences?" Kristen says.

"Are you chopping someone's head off?" Mary says.

We stand in the school corridor between classes, Lisa, Mary, Kristen, Melanie and me. Mary and Kristen are sisters. Melanie is my closest friend here at the school. I've known these girls for a short time, only nine months since my parents moved to Warren from Cape Cod. Our homes are right next door to each other over on Spring Street.

My name is Kate Walker, my friends call me Katie, and I just had my fourteenth birthday last Saturday. I attend Barrington High School and I'm in the ninth grade, a freshman.

The girls surround me before my open locker during third period. I came to school with this large bag on wheels that I carry my fencing gear in. I've got to practice after school at the Rhode Island Fencing Academy and Club. By their questions I know they have no real idea what fencing is. Because the U.S. team did so well, they had a few glimpses of the sport when the summer

13

Olympics were on TV. But even then, so few bouts were televised that my friends never really got into it.

Although my friends' questions are a little surprising, knowing that I wouldn't be engaged in such activities as chopping off heads and putting up picket fences, I am patient with them.

"Show us your equipment," Lisa says, pointing to the bag.

From the bag I pull out a mask, a jacket, an underarm protector, knee-length pants called knickers, a glove, fencing sneakers and my weapons, what nonfencers call "swords."

I have three epees. I prefer the epee over the foil and the saber. I like the epee because it requires deep concentration on the part of the fencer. It makes me think more. My coach says it fits my personality to a "T."

"Wow! That's cool," Kristen says, holding up a blade.

"Tell us more about it," Mary begs as she admires the mask. "What *exactly* is fencing, anyway?"

I love to talk about fencing, and their questions give me the opportunity to do so. I've been involved with fencing since I was eight.

I tell them that fencing is like an animated chess game, an intense game of calculation and shrewd cunning between two knowing opponents, who move up and down a long, narrow playing field called a strip, trying to score points on each other. Only it's much, much faster. The game takes constant planning, and courage to go on the offensive and not allow yourself to be intimidated by your opponent's tricks and traps. I just have to calculate what my opponent is up to, what she is thinking and planning, but it all happens in a matter of seconds. Fencing keeps me on my toes.

I also tell them that being engaged in a fencing bout on a strip is like being transferred back into some romantic time where duels were conducted on a field of honor. I find that fencing is classier than any other sport that I've been involved in. For me, fencing is a game for gentlemen and ladies, and being part of the sport gives me the sense that I'm doing something honorable.

I play chess with my father a lot, too. He taught me the rules of the game at the age of six. Chess is a game of strategy and tac-

Katie warms up.

tics. I kind of like to compare the sport of fencing to a game of chess because you first have to know how each piece can move. When you know what all the chess pieces can do, when you learn the basic moves and build on them, then you're ready for strategy. Fencing is like that.

Some of the rules of chess can be applied to fencing. I look at my opponent's moves, determine what sort of plan she has based on how she plays, and then I make the best countermove possible. I always have to have a plan of my own and I am always on the alert because just a moment's distraction may cost me a point. And I don't ever rush into a crazy move or I'll blow it real quickly.

Fencing is a very challenging game. It always leaves me exhausted, but I don't forget to have fun, remembering that I'm doing something I really love.

"You sure sound like you love fencing a lot," Lisa declares, trying on the mask.

All that, plus it's lots of fun. More fun than any other sport.

I tell her it's thrilling to be a fencer, and I love the excitement of swordplay. Fencing is a lot of quick thinking on my feet. It's also good for my mind and the exercise is good for my body. And truly, it inspires the spirit. It teaches me the values of discipline. It clears my mind of day-to-day problems; it helps me to focus on the present and to react quickly to situations. I can be a better fencer with lots of training.

"But with all that training, when do you have time to do anything else? When do you get to study?" Kristen asks.

Since I took up fencing, I've done so much better in school, especially with problem-solving, which is a large part of the sport. My grades and test scores are so much better, too. My mind doesn't drift as much as before because of my ability to focus, which I've gained through fencing. The action of fencing starts in the mind. It becomes a real intellectual game because of the strategic planning.

"You get all that from fencing? I never knew it," Melanie says.

"But is it really, really safe?" Kristen asks.

It's one of the safest competitive sports around. Sure I get hit a lot, it's part of the game, but remember, I'm wearing a lot of protective clothing. Without warming up properly, I may get an occasional sprain, or I may even pull a few muscles with my lunges. I do admit I get an occasional black-and-blue mark on my arm or leg because of the point of the blade hitting my body.

"What's the object of the game?" Mary asks. "I mean, what are you trying to do?"

The object of fencing in a **bout**, that's what an individual game or match between two fencers is called, is to score points by making touches with your weapon: five points in preliminary pool play or fifteen points in direct elimination play.

"What is the first thing you learn as a fencer, Katie?" Lisa asks.

That fencing is a lot of hard work; it requires both dedication and resilience. I learn to fence as a dancer learns to dance. A duel is like a dance number and it's just as cool. I have to focus on exactly what I'm doing, concentrate on what *I'm* doing and what my *opponent's* doing. But most of all, fencing requires practice, practice and more practice if I am going to make it.

"Who wants to do all that?" Kristen grins. "I hate to exercise."

Once you get into it—and I promise you—you will, you'll get hooked, and you will even notice that you are having a good workout. It'll make you feel good. It relieves the stress of the day. Just imagine all the fun and excitement of being a fencer. And it's really cool to say to someone, "I'm a fencer!"

There's something so thrilling when I enter the Club and hear that sound of steel against steel, the tap-tap of blades. It's some kind of magic, a magic I haven't yet identified, but when I do hear it, I know I am entering a whole new world that most people don't know about. When I first hear that sound and haven't expected it, it gets me excited, it makes my blood start pumping. I just want to get suited up and start fencing.

"Isn't fencing a boy's sport?" Melanie asks.

Oh, no! Once you put on that mask, everyone's the same, all gender is lost. Boys and girls are treated equally. The most important qualities of fencing are who you are and what skills you can learn. You learn respect for your teammates and for the sport. As you become a fencer, you learn that fencing is not simply a game with rules, but a classic sport of honor and courage that you must take seriously, especially regarding your safety. Safety is always first.

"You sure make it sound exciting," Lisa says. "You think we can do it?"

I tell them I know they can.

I see how excited they are getting over the sport. I tell them that I enjoy fencing because it's both an individual and a team sport. Fencers compete as individuals and in team events. That's why fencing is so great for me. We train together as a team. We really get that friendship. I like the team spirit, but it's nice to have my own drive.

"I thought fencing was a lot of fancy clothes, swinging from chandeliers or leaping from balconies," Mary says.

That's just the stuff of movies, all drama and high jinks. But it sure makes the sport attractive. I tell them to come to one of my training sessions at the Club on Tournament Tuesday to see for themselves. Tournament Tuesday is an informal competition for club members that are held every Tuesday night.

You really have to want to fence; you can't just go to class and go through the motions. You have to really want to go through the training, which is hard, and you have to stick with it. You can judge for yourself if fencing is right for you.

"What do you fight for now?"
"I fight for the belief that every man can be better"
— The Man in the Iron Mask: 1998

The Island Fencing Academy, Warren, Rhode Island

The store and enrollment center.

HONOR

to be on a team...

I am a member of the Rhode Island Fencing Academy and Club in Warren. It was founded in 1994 and is a well-respected school because it helps to develop athletes for competition. The Academy's goal is to build up each individual through the challenge of fencing by instilling in him or her self-confidence, coordination, concentration and etiquette, while teaching them all aspects of the history of the sword. And to have fun doing it!

The season for competitive fencers runs from September to the first week in July, but the Academy is open all year round.

Almost all Academy staff are fencers. Alex Ripa is RIFAC'S founder and head coach. Jill Ripa is my coach and the Academy's director. Both Alex and Jill are certified fencing instructors. Jill is also an occupational therapist and Alex comes from art school.

Jill makes the whole show run; she's the one who answers all the questions. She's also a very intense coach, even though she makes fencing look very easy.

The Academy also has a program coordinator. She runs the day-to-day operations of the Academy, including class registrations and running the fencing supply store. She signs me up for a Junior Bouting class that meets every Wednesday. When I go home I'll tell Mom and Dad that I signed up and that I need money to pay for the class, and I'll get their written consent. My class will meet once a week for six weeks.

My goal this year is to fence at the national championships and win a medal. I've come a long way through my training from when I first started to fence. As a team member today and as a competitive fencer, I look fondly back on my early days training in classes, first in foil, then in epee. My father drove me from Cape Cod to Warren just to take the classes. Jill was my trainer back then, too. We have a great friendship!

I remember my first day at the Academy. I was taking the Youth Beginning class for ages 8-13. I was eight. My heart was pumping fast, and I was so nervous and yet very excited by the prospect of being part of a new adventure.

Jill blew her whistle. All the students lined up in a straight line. All the boys hung together on one side, and all the girls on the other side.

"Are you guys ready to jump in?" Jill said.

We began our fifteen-minute warm-up. I rarely exercised at home, and I found the many exercises very strenuous. We did this every time before we practiced. Once we had memorized the warm-ups, we were more or less left on our own. Now I use music while warming up. I put on my head phones and listen to music that has a beat to it to

Gloves, underarm protectors, weapons and jackets

Masks and weapons waiting to be selected

pump me up and get me in the mood. Music helps motivate me. But that first day, I didn't have the music. My heart was pumping me up all on its own.

We followed our exercises by getting into an "en garde" position, thrusting our imaginary weapons out, using first the right foot in front of us, then our left foot, as we moved across the room. We did several stationary exercises to loosen our legs — knee bends, then running in place while bending our knees. Then came a kind of frog bending exercise; we stretched low, crisscrossed our ankles left over the right, right over the left, and then did a few push-ups.

Jill blew her whistle again. She told us to take a sip of water and gather again on one side of the room. She told us about the awards several of the students received while fencing in competitions in the New England area over the past week.

In the class that followed that first day, we learned the basic positions or stances and the first footwork techniques. Eighty percent of the game is footwork. We also learned how to hold the weapon, plus a little fencing history. By the fourth meeting, we began basic bouting and learned how a bout is organized. Everybody began with the foil. When I graduated from the beginner class, I felt comfortable and confident fencing in bouts.

I treasure those early days and think of them often. They remind me of who I was and how far I've come. Those comforting thoughts of the progress I've made keep me focused.

The word **fencing** comes from the words "offense" and "defense," and in modern fencing athletes use both to achieve victory. In foil fencing one fencer may **attack** and the other may parry with her weapon. A **parry** is a motion made to deflect or block your opponent's oncoming blade. Using distinctive footwork to stay at a safe distance, a fencer

Katie Walker and Maddy Buxton

may decide to launch an attack of her own. She may also attack into her opponent's attack, creating a **counterattack**, and if she surprises her opponent, scores, and escapes being touched, then she gets the point. It is like a dance between two opponents, but at a very fast speed.

I go to the movies all the time. I first got exposed to fencing at the movies. I love costumes and costume drama, pageantry, historical stories, stories about honor and chivalry, knighthood and adventure. And, of course, romance. I guess I'm a true romantic at heart. You see, my father is a movie projectionist and he owns and runs a revival movie house with my mother over in Templeton. I get to see the movies for free. I've always loved Errol Flynn and Tyrone Power, both screen duelers of the 1930s and 1940s because they were always fighting duels with the likes of evil Basil Rathbone. The neat thing about these movie stars is that they did their own fencing. They were excellent fencers in their own right, which made the magic up there on the screen seem even more real.

Many cultures, including the Italian, French and even the Spanish, developed unique styles of fencing, but during the Renaissance all three created the discipline in fencing that took on an aura of high drama, with the fencing masters refining their secret and historical techniques and passing them on to the world.

The world of fencing fascinates me. I'm very, very eager to learn all I can about fencing and all that fencing entails, especially its history and its pageantry.

The first thing I learned in that beginning class was to salute one another before we practiced. **Saluting** is a way to show the proper respect to your opponent and to your coach and referee. You salute before practice and at the end of practice, before a bout and after a bout. Then you get in the ready position. In the **ready position**, you stand in an L-shaped position, with one foot forward and the other

perpendicular to it, the heels together with your legs straight. Next you bring the bell guard up to your chin, then bring the point down at an angle to the floor with a slight bow of the head if you want to, just like in the movies.

En garde, which literally means "on guard," is a fencing position or stance that fencers assume before they play. After the game, you must give a handshake to your opponent, using the hand that is weapon-free.

I always find that learning fencing terminology is very difficult; there are so many moves to know and so many words to know that identify the moves. It is like learning a whole new language and most of it is in French! I find it very demanding.

In the beginner's class, we worked on the fencing strip and learned how to move up and down it, using our footwork. We also learned how to stand, how to advance, lunge and retreat, and how to always remain balanced in our position. I tried to keep calm and learn to breathe during all those moves, concentrating on what Jill was saying all the time. I tried to build up my self-confidence by persisting in my training and never giving up, although my legs and knees and arms were at times screaming for me to stop.

Jill said, "Advance-extend-lunge-recover-en garde."

There was a lot of stress on my knees those first days, but during practice you built up and developed the power in your legs and lower body.

Jill worked closely with us as a group, then in groups of three, then with each of us individually, depending on our needs. The philosophy of the coaching staff is to treat each individual with a lot of respect. A lot of the kids in that class came from team sports where they were not treated well by their former teammates and coaches. But they did well in fencing because it's such an individual sport. They felt kind of special doing it, too.

One of the first things I learned in that class, before I actually had a weapon in my hand, was to think of my fingers as the tip of my blade. As I advanced toward my opponent, my eyes focused on my target area, I extended my arm, lunged, and then recovered. My opponent moved according to my moves, trying to keep safe, all the while trying to find the distance to launch her own attack.

We learned that the first line of defense was to retreat.

What I found difficult at first was the **double advance** or **double retreat,** which helped me to gain or give ground quickly. It's like two advances but without the pause in between. What I found difficult was that I had to first advance at normal speed, and then my second advance was faster. But with hard work, I finally got it.

I also learned **distance-keeping**. I can do this by simply touching my opponent's hand with mine to keep an even distance between us in our advances and retreats while fencing.

Jill told us there were three distances to maintain: arm-extension distance, lunge distance and advance-lunge distance.

She also told us that timing was important, more than speed. If the timing was right, the speed would come.

After a brief lesson and workout, Jill told us to take a sip of water. Half the students dropped their foils and masks to the floor and retreated to the sidelines for water or Gatorade. The drink was sure a welcomed relief. You can't imagine how parched I got!

When I worked with Jill, she tapped my weapon's blade as a prompt to recover as we practiced a particular move. She was very thorough and articulate, and the practice was intense.

To keep the curve in my blade or to straighten it a bit more, I used my sneaker and ran it down the blade. Sometimes I just kept bending or flexing my weapon to keep its curve.

Two hearts for target practice

Crossed swords

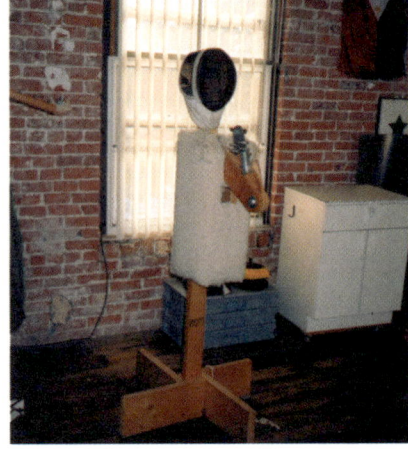

The mannequin

We kept changing our opponents in practice so we learned to adapt to different opponents.

Jill constantly reminded us to bend our knees, to keep our front foot forward and our shoulders and back straight. She told us this over and over again because we always forgot it. It was important to keep our upper carriage and balance centered so weren't leaning forward or backward. We also had to remember to keep our rear arm back, to keep it out of the way. It helped us maintain our balance as well.

My body ached all the time during those early days because my muscles were getting a real workout.

We also learned to use our breath effectively. When we lunged, we exhaled to make sure we didn't hold our breath. We learned to coordinate our breathing by inhaling and exhaling. You'll be surprised how many of us forgot to breathe.

I usually set a goal for myself during each practice. I try to work on a particular skill and use it when I go into competition. I'm always checking the bulletin board for competitions. I tend to get undisciplined if I don't set a goal.

I try hard to be a better fencer; there are lots of ways to diversify and increase my training and to keep moving along the path of a fencer. There are good role models here at the Club and I try to emulate them. I train with the coaches and with students who are at a higher level than me. They get me excited by their fencing style, like some of the older girls and guys who have already achieved a certain level of fencing I want to get to.

I've grown stronger physically; I have a long reach and strong legs and I try to use them to my advantage.

I practice at home two hours a week, twenty minutes a day. I go to the Academy three times a week to practice, working on my footwork, parrying strategies, advances and lunges. I really, really like to take my opponent's blade with circle six, a circular sweep of my blade, before I hit her. I love doing that because it's stylish and fun. I like being aggressive.

In the beginning, Jill told us some things to think about while we're training. She told us to watch ourselves and others, to think before we do anything, even though we have to think quickly. She emphasized that we have to respect each other on and off the playing field, and not just hope to react to the opponent's actions. She taught us to have a plan during a bout. Commitment to your chosen move is most important. If you're not committed, you risk losing control of the bout.

Alex and Jill know how to make me feel good about what I do in class. They want me to enjoy what I'm doing and what I'm trying to do, and they recognize the goals I set for myself. They also recognize my individual struggles as I learn how to hold my weapon and to move, and all the frustrations that go with learning this or any sport. And they take the time to encourage me to go on and compliment me when I do well. It all comes down to self-sacrifice and grace under pressure.

Alex is strict and he knows how to push me, but not push me too far, because he knows my personal limitations. He knows how to make me work hard during practice, because he knows who I am and what I'm capable of achieving. It's a good balance. He tries to bring the best out of me. I want him to bring the best out of me. The best thing about him is his a great sense of humor. His sense of humor allows me to get to know him more on a personal level. He's a really cool coach.

Katie with Kathryn Hawrot

So is Jill. She's lively and animated and sincerely wants me to achieve my goals. Someday I'll make fencing look very easy, just like she does!

I learned that concentration, keeping calm, stamina, persistence, self-confidence and sportsmanship are all important in fencing.

Fencing gives me an edge. If I were to quit, I would lose that edge. I feel like I'm carrying a lot more weight on my shoulders these days with fencing, school, ballet, theater, kung fu, and the responsibility that goes with all of it. The qualities and characteristics I have acquired these past months cannot be replaced. I truly love what I do.

Katie and the fencing team

Gloves, underarm protectors, weapons and jackets

Great friends! Katie Walker and Ariel Gitlin

CHOICE
of a weapon...

Some students choose to develop their skills in all three weapons, but most compete in one. I chose the epee. Both Alex and Jill believe I will do well with the epee.

There are two kinds of fencing. **Electric fencing** is for competitions and practice on club nights. Fencers are electrically hooked up to a scoring board, making it much easier for a referee to know to whom to award the touch. But much more on this later.

Dry fencing is for drilling. We use dry fencing in class; there's no electric gear. We're watched by our classmates who act as officials. We all take turns doing this and fencing. We concentrate on our footwork, our stance, and how to hold our weapon. Sometimes we don't even keep score, which makes it easier to learn our techniques and not worry about who is winning.

As I practice, I learn how to hold my weapon, move with it, attack with it, defend myself with it, touch the target area of my opponent with it, and defend myself from being touched with my opponent's weapon.

On the first day, I studied the various parts of the weapon. I found this study very exciting. It was good to know all about the weapons I was using. Each weapon has a grip, either a French grip or a Pistol grip. A **French**

Masks and weapons waiting to be selected

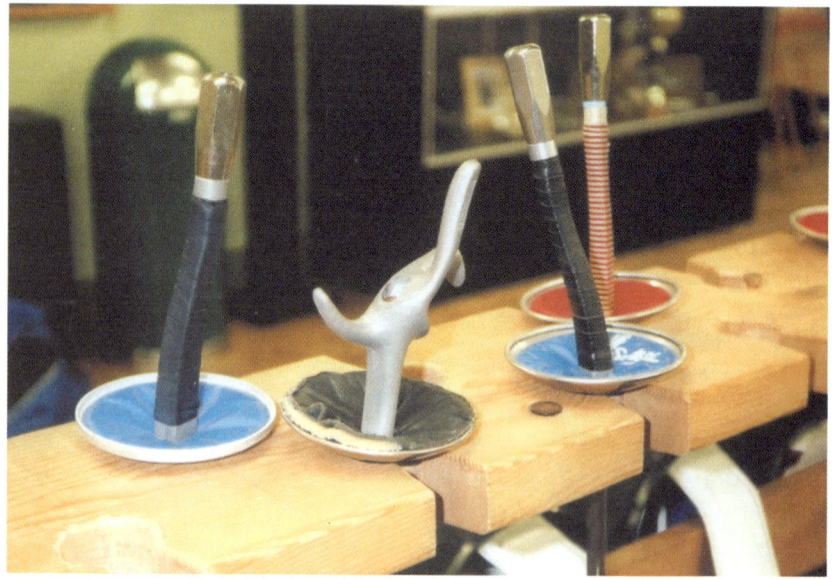

French grips and Pistol grip

grip is long, slightly curved, and looks like a regular sword handle. It is designed either for a right-handed or a left-handed fencer. I'm a right-handed fencer, and I find that I have more trouble with left-handed fencers during a bout than with right-handed fencers.

Instead of a French grip, a foil or epee might have a **Pistol grip**, which is a molded shape that fits your hand. I like the pistol grip better because it is more versatile; it allows me to do a lot more things with my hand. However, it takes a lot more training on the student's part because beginners tend to hold the whole pistol grip in their hand like a club.

I started with a French grip over the other grips because it really forced me to use my fingers to control my weapon. I eventually worked my way to a Pistol grip, which I find is much more comfortable.

A **pommel** is the large heavy nut at the bottom of the handle when a French grip is used. It helps to balance the weapon.

A **guard** is the bowl-shaped circle of metal that protects your hand. It is padded inside. In the epee, the guard is larger than the foil's to allow more protection for the hand, since the hand is part of the target. In the saber, the guard is U-shaped and protects the whole hand.

The **blade** is the stabbing or cutting part of the sword. It has four parts: the **forte** is the thick part of the blade nearest the guard; the **center** is the middle of the blade; the **foible** is the top and thinnest part of the blade. And lastly is the **point** or tip. On the foil, the point is buttoned and covered with a rubber tip for dry fencing. In electric fencing, you have a spring-loaded tip on the foil and epee that is electrically wired.

Jill gives us a little history on the sport of fencing. Modern fencing is a mixture of many schools of fencing, but is primarily influenced by the Italian and French school. Each school has had its share of great fencing masters, too:

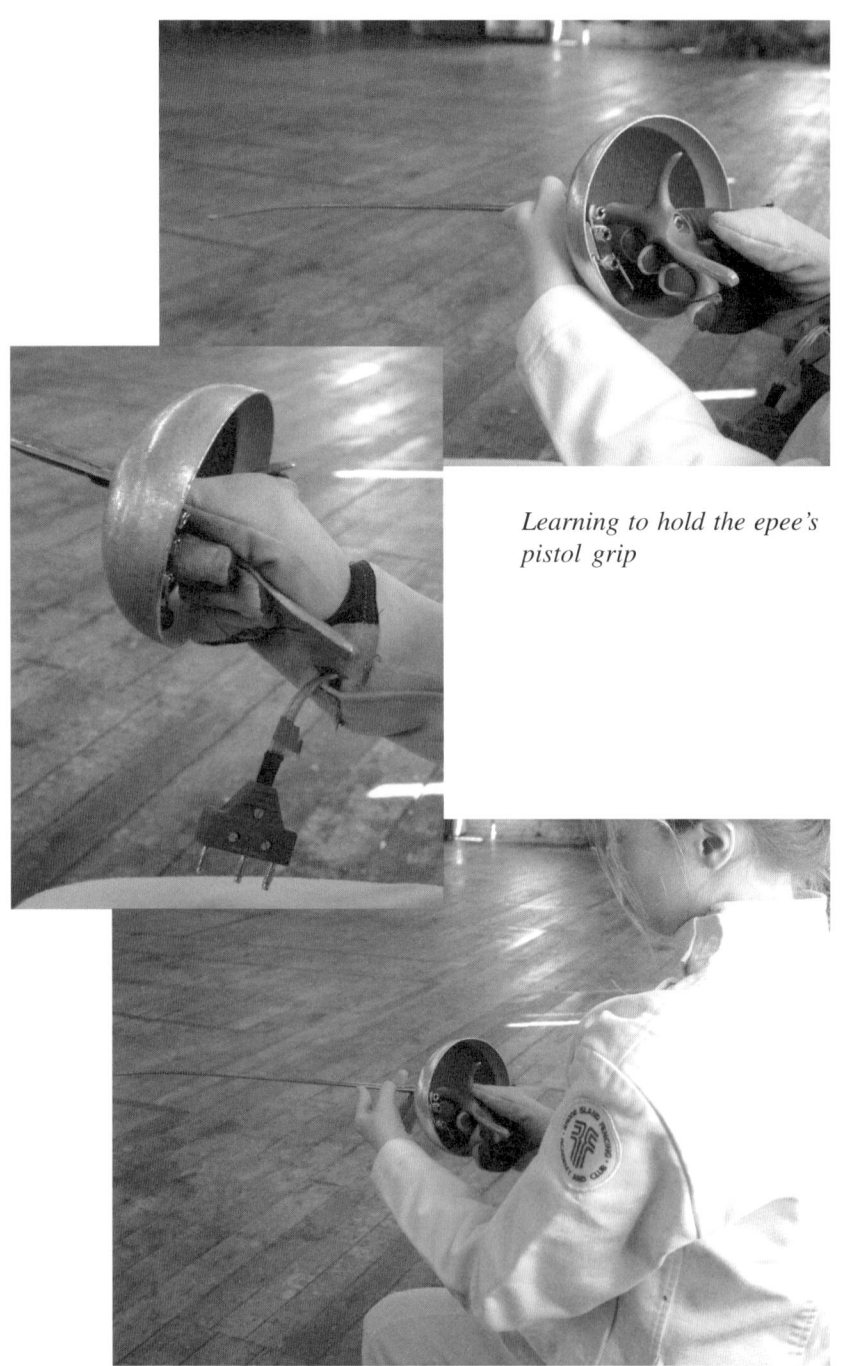

Learning to hold the epee's pistol grip

men like Greco, Pini, Pessina and Nadi in Italy; Kirchoffer, Merignac, Rue and Gaudin in France. Lots of other countries have influenced fencing. Recently, Eastern European countries have made many contributions. I've always liked the international and exotic element of the sport.

Sword fighting is one of the oldest sports in existence. It dates back at least to ancient Egypt. Modern fencing sprang from the duel, evolving in the sixteenth century. In the old days, swords were used in combat as a means of settling questions of justice or of vindicating a grievance. Duels were used to settle matters of a legal nature or a matter of honor. Sometimes people fought over a simple insult or over a woman's honor. In some duels, honor was satisfied when blood was first drawn. In others, duelists fought until one combatant was dead. It seemed they cared more for their honor than their lives. And some people literally lost their lives over an insult. Honor was the thing.

In the mid-nineteenth century, dueling went on the decline as means of settling scores between men and women because your victory could land you in jail with charges of assault or manslaughter. It was soon decided that it was best to defeat your opponent instead of killing him. Duels often ended just by wounding someone. There would be fewer legal problems for the duelists. All in all, dueling soon faded after the First World War.

Training with the sword helped you stand a little taller, and hopefully be a more organized and logical person, or at least a safer person. Jill says the old days were a time when everyone carried a sword on their belt, much like the Old West when everyone carried a gun. If you carried a sword you were expected to know how to use it. So it was in your interest to perfect your skills with the sword. Your life depended on it!

There are three weapons used in modern fencing. They are the foil, the epee and the saber.

EN GARDE!

The Fencing Lesson with Epee. *Katie Walker, the student, and her coach, Jill Ripa. Jill wears a coaching plastron.*

Getting into an "en garde" position

44

En garde!

Parry six

Lunge to chest

There are a couple of things about the **foil** that are still really important in the game today. One is that the foil is a point-thrusting weapon and was developed as a training weapon back in the days of dueling. Points are scored with the tip of the blade only and must land within the torso of the body of the opponent. It does not include the arms, neck, head, legs or feet. Any touches or contact made with the edge of the foil are ignored by the referee. The 18th-century fencing masters instructed their pupils to attack only the vital areas of the body.

An important rule in foil and saber fencing is something called the **right-of-way**. It is a system of offense and defense that allows the referee to figure out who has the right to earn a point when the fencers have both landed hits during the same action. Only the fencer who began his attack gets the point if he hits a valid target area. The fencer who is being attacked must parry or block that attack and not allow the attacker to hit. A fencer who hesitates too long while moving on the attack might just give up her right-of-way to her opponent. No points are awarded if a referee determines that both fencers began to attack at the same time, and they start again.

The **epee** is a direct descendent of the dueling sword. With the epee the whole body is the target. That includes from the top of the mask to the toe, including the hands, so there are no off-target areas. There is no right-of-way with the epee.

Like the foil, the epee is only a thrusting weapon. The epee is styled more after the weapons that were used back in the days of dueling when a simple touch or nick would draw blood. Only touches scored with the point of the weapon count for points.

The epee is similar in length to the foil, but is heavier and has a much stiffer, thicker blade.

Foil fencing at practice

Epee fencing at practice

Sabre fencing at practice

Beginning to lunge

Lunge conclusion

I like the epee best because it forces you to be patient when you fence. You have to think and plan out your timing before you attack your opponent. I find it's more of a challenge, and your reactions have to be instantaneous because you can be hit anywhere.

The **saber** is the only cutting weapon in modern fencing, which means you can score points with the blade's edges. The saber is a modern version of the slashing cavalry sword tradition. Soldiers on horseback would fight with sabers. So, to represent that tradition in the modern games the target is limited to the head, torso, arms, and all the way down to the waist of your opponent, much like the cavalry rider on a horse. Everything below the waist is off-limits.

You can also score with the point of the saber, but fencers mostly use the edge.

Saber fencing has right-of-way, just like the foil. It also has a lot of the back-and-forth action seen in countless movies, rather than whoever hits first, like in epee. The fencer who starts the attack first is given priority should his opponent counterattack. Sometimes you see a saber fencer make a move called a **stop cut** against his opponent's forearm during a moment's hesitation, winning right-of-way and the point.

All three weapons are fenced electrically, and when you get to a certain point in your training, you may train with each weapon. However, a year of foil fencing is required by the Academy before you can go on to the other two.

During training, Alex and Jill watch you and monitor your fencing style. They kind of size you up to see what weapon is best suited for you. It must be a good match, like a good marriage, between the student's personality and the characteristics of the weapon she trains with. It is obvious to the student and the coach when it is not a good match.

Fleche

Choosing a weapon is also based a lot on body type. Everyone in the class is different. Some of us are tall, some of us are short, some are heavier or skinnier, so it makes a lot of sense to find the perfect match between student and weapon. Jill says very tall people tend to do better in epee because reach really matters when you're trying to hit first.

Foil fencers also have a certain temperament, and they tend to be a mixture of both epee and saber fencers.

Epee fencers tend to be very logical and very calculating on the strip, but patient, waiting for the right move, while saber users tend to plan quickly and act very fast.

When you get to a certain level in fencing, it all boils down to the psychology of it and your physical ability to back up your moves.

A student must have heart behind her weapon. And passion!

"We all believed we should spend our lives in the service of something more than ourselves"

– The Man in the Iron Mask: 1998

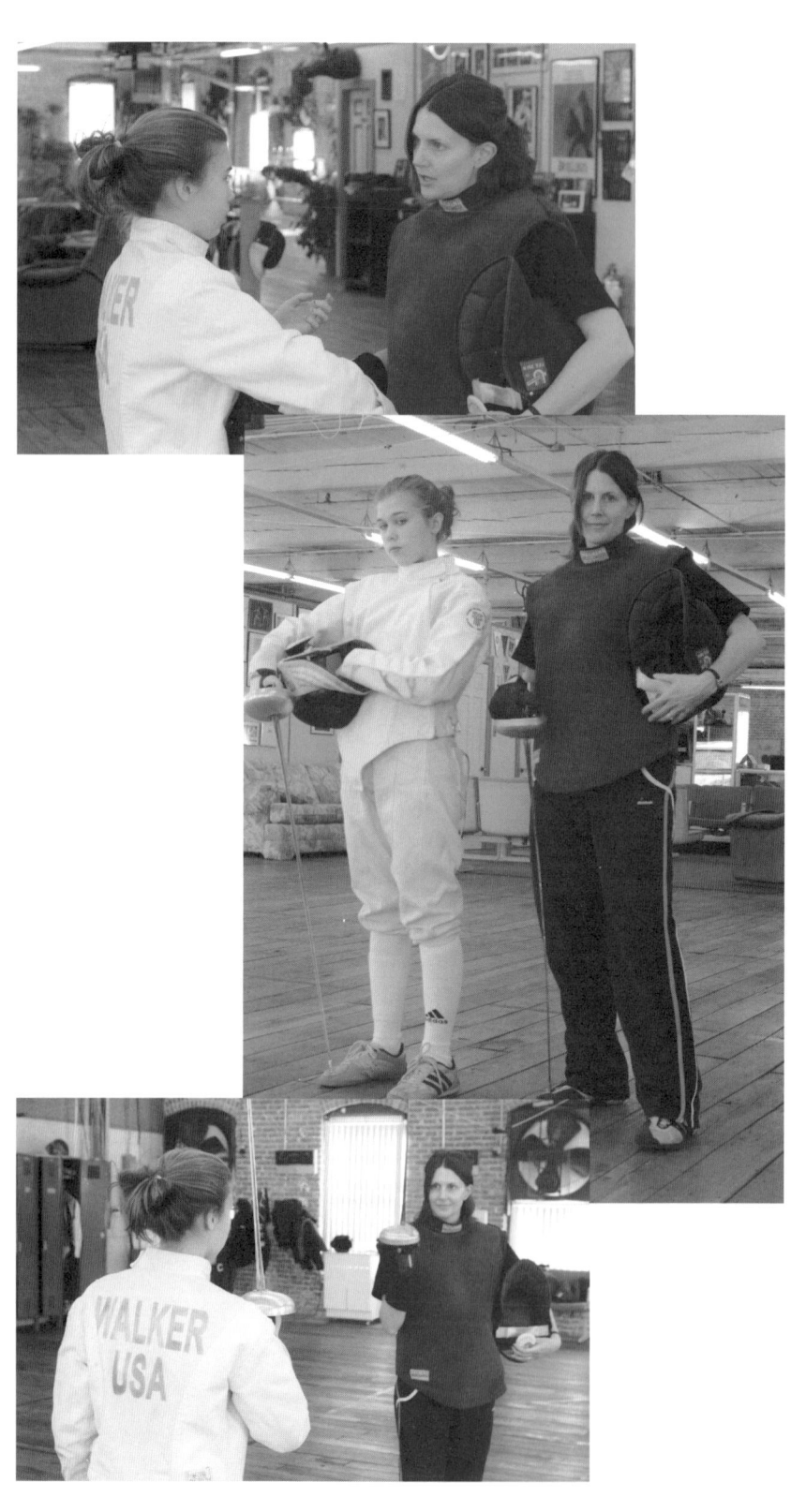

CONFIDENCE

in yourself...

I try to work out at home on days I don't have fencing class. I do stretching exercises, sit-ups and deep knee-bends. I also practice in front of a full-length mirror in my room to see if I'm standing properly, reminding myself to keep my back straight. If anything, fencing has taught me that I'd better be in good shape or else I'll never make it. Fencing is a very strenuous undertaking.

I arrange to meet Lori, another competitor and a good, close friend, in the park after school, and we go for a run together to build up our endurance and strength because they are such big parts of fencing. If you don't have enough endurance, you get tired real fast at practice. But the strenuous exercise makes you feel good. It also relieves the stress of the day, especially a school day, and during exams.

I like school a lot, but right now, since it's my first year in high school, I have to take the required courses, such as math, history, science and a language. I'm learning French this year and it's real difficult, but it helps me with those French fencing terms! I'd like to go to France someday. But my favorite subject is history. Especially world history.

I also belong to the school's theater program. I like acting best, being on stage, being a presence, being part of the experience of the moment.

On the Strip. *Preparing to fence*

Parrying an attack to the foot

Stop-touch to the mask

*Riposte to
the leg*

55

I remember my first time on stage. I was in a play called *A Christmas Carol*. I only had a few lines. I was so afraid that I wouldn't remember my lines, my stomach was in knots during rehearsal. I almost couldn't go out on stage on opening night, but the cast knew this was my first time, and they cheered me on. I used all that pent-up energy, fear and anxiousness to my advantage, and somehow, when I finally got on the stage, I forgot there was a paying audience out there and I managed to get through the scene. I was able to say all my lines correctly and even managed to put a little emotion behind some of the lines and make it work for me. I only got better with each performance. Fencing is like that, sometimes. Persistence and courage to do the hard work pays off in the end.

Fencing taught me to work well with people. My friends and I spend so much time together, and we get along so well together, they are really a second family to me.

Both fencers protect their legs.

I also take kung fu classes once a week and ballet and jazz lessons twice a week. These activities complement my fencing work. I've grown stronger, physically and emotionally, because of these activities.

Kung fu means "a disciplined person." I like to think of myself as a disciplined person. I want to be a disciplined person. I set a goal for myself and try to achieve it by a certain date. I'm also diligent about my classes, being there on time, listening to my coaches, and practicing later at home what I learned in class.

My instructor, Victor Wu, talks about the concept of yin and yang. He believes it is the essence of all martial arts. The yin and yang emblem shows the two opposing forces or energies at work. Mr. Wu says you need both to make an even balance in the nature of things. Yin is the passive or yielding force, always identified as the female force. Yang is the active or assertive force, always identified as the male force.

The same principles can be applied to the sport of fencing. The aggressor is the one on the attack, and the opponent is the one on the defensive. Then they switch places. The opponent becomes the aggressor, and the attacker goes on the defensive. They balance each other out. Fencing needs both opposing forces to maintain the back-and-forth action, which is what fencing is all about.

Mr. Wu says martial arts is more about stances and different ways to shift your body and going for the hit. We don't move side to side in fencing as in martial arts. You have more fixed positions than in fencing. You learn to shift your weight back and forth, front leg to back leg, but in fencing you don't do that. You move your whole body as a unit, and that makes the transition from martial arts to fencing harder.

Many people think fencing is more like martial arts, but it's probably more like ballet. Ballet helps students to be light and quick on their feet. You learn how to move, lift up on your body and not be so heavy on your feet. Fencing is much like a dance, anyway.

My ballet instructor, Miss Ginger, who was once a great ballerina in her time, says ballet deals with control, learning body awareness and how to move your body well. Jill agrees that in ballet you use a lot of your core muscles which are very good to build up your strength, muscles that I use in fencing, especially to keep my back straight. I think that for ballet, the control of movement is key.

When I fence with my friends, I don't hold back, and I expect the same from them. Lori and I both give it our all. That helps us to challenge ourselves. I do myself and her justice by giving her a good fight. We have to focus on hitting the target. I don't think about her as being my friend. I don't think about hurting her. Respect plays a big part in this. We all love to make it work. We have to have trust in our teammates.

At home, Dad went up into the attic and brought down an old mannequin that Mom used to sew dresses on. I think it is from the 1940s. Dad attached a fencing mask to the head, made a flexible arm, and attached an epee to the fake hand. He designed a padded heart and attached it to its chest. I practice my lunges and hits on it. It helps to build up my stamina, my aim and my form. I also like an opponent who can't hit back!

Dad also made up this contraption for me which has a golf ball suspended on a string from the ceiling to the floor with the ball in the middle. I use it to practice using my fingers and concentrating on hitting the ball with the point of my blade. It is very difficult for me to hit the ball.

Sometimes I sit with Dad in the living room and watch old fencing movies together. Dad makes popcorn for us. Tonight we are watching *Scaramouche*, which features the

Attack to the leg

Riposte to the body

Touch to the body

longest swordfight in movie history. Then we have a good game of chess before going to bed. Dad wins again, but it is a great challenge to try to outsmart him. That's one of my goals, to win a game of chess with my dad.

Dad gives me the drive to be the best I can be in the choices I make. Mom makes sure I have everything I need to win.

On Tuesday nights, I go to Club Night at the Academy. Club Nights are nights that RIFAC sets aside especially for experienced fencers. I get a chance to relax, fence with my friends or make new acquaintances, talk with the coaches and ask them questions, and generally have some fun while meeting new opponents. Everyone is usually open and always willing to say "hello" and introduce themselves. It's a very friendly atmosphere.

When you're new, it might make you kind of nervous because there are so many things going on all at once. You don't know who to ask what to do, where to go; you are generally left on your own. It can be really nerve-wracking to be the new guy or gal. But you soon learn that you are welcomed here.

Lisa, Mary, Kristen and Melanie come with me to Club Night to see what fencing is really like. They have a good time, but only Melanie signs up for a beginner class. I guess fencing is not for everyone.

Open fencing is just that: open for everyone. It gives me an opportunity to work on my skills on the strip and generally have some fun while working out. I really like fencing with the guys. A lot of them are much stronger and more challenging than someone at my own level. They like to take many risks, so it's really fun to try new things against them. I am sometimes successful, but they really want to win, which only makes me work harder. A couple of older boys who are more experienced than me, Henry and Frank, really give me a workout. I don't like fencing

Mid-attack

Refereeing a bout

Waiting to fence

with students my own age and skill level because it doesn't provide me with the same challenge as the older boys do.

Every Tuesday, RIFAC hosts Tournament Tuesday. This weekly event is open to any Club member in any weapon. On Tournament Tuesday, a pool-format tournament is made up of all the fencers who have come to participate in each weapon. Final placements are recorded and awards are given out quarterly to the Club member with the best record.

I have a tremendous sense of accomplishment when I hit parts of the target that I find really hard to get. Right now, I am working on one thing that is really troubling me, and that is hitting my opponent's foot. The more I work on toe touches, the better I will remember it. It boosts my confidence when I am able to achieve something difficult.

On Thursday nights at RIFAC, Junior Bouting for ages 13-16 is held. This class is an hour and a half long and is an opportunity to meet and fence with other RIFAC members in your age group. The class features lots of electric fencing and lots of feedback from the coach.

Friday nights, RIFAC features open fencing all night. Alex says it's a night of fencing that can be as challenging or as fun as the opponent you choose. When you enjoy what you are doing and trying to do, you get better through the experience.

You belong to only one club, one team. You represent your club. That makes us a very tight-knit group. I'm glad I belong to RIFAC.

"You wouldn't care to transfer that feeling into action, would you?"
— The Mark of Zorro: 1940

Refereeing the bout

Touch to the shoulder

COMMITMENT

to the sport...

In July, I go to Youth Camp at the Academy. Youth Camp is always a lot of fun. It is a full-day camp for beginners, as well as experienced and competitive fencers. There's a lot of fencing going on and fencing-specific games and drills. Alex says beginners get a solid fencing foundation from this experience and the more experienced fencers greatly improve their performance and techniques.

Alex and his staff guide the kids every step of the way. In the morning there are always workshops and games, blade work and structured bouting, even a fencing movie. In the afternoon there's open fencing and tournament practice, then a cooling-down session. Friday of each week is Tournament Day.

Although I think it's so cool when I tell people I am a fencer, I find I have to explain what fencing actually is. This is a common complaint among fencers who have to endure those puzzled expressions on people's faces when you say you fence. We just have to be patient with all the questions because we want to change their negative perception of the sport. We're proud of our sport, and we want to share the fun we get from it with everyone.

During the Olympics, the networks didn't televise the bouts often enough. They needed to do pieces on the com-

Quinn Crum learning to referee

Jeff Mooney, coach, and Anna Pet, student, and Renee Heitman, student

petitors, who the champions were, their training, about their families, and how they got to their level. Just like they do with the athletes in all the other sports.

I have a neat collection of fencing movies at home, mostly the classics by MGM or Warner Bros. But instructional fencing DVD's and videos are few and too specialized for the casual viewer, limited to the people who actually do the sport. There are no fencing equipment stores in the malls like other sporting good stores, nor are there sign-up booths with representatives from the sport or the schools who teach it, or school advertisements highlighting the sport. I think it's sad the public has not been given the chance to know what fencing is all about. This is very discouraging. I think the movies and a few commercials on TV have been the only source of exposure for the sport. If the public saw tournaments regularly on TV like other spectator sports, they would know what it is like; they might even become interested in becoming a fencer once they learn its various components and learn how much fun it is.

Fencers today need so much of a mind-body connection to pull it off for the long term. We should enjoy the game for its intrinsic values. I realize this all the time. I must have a positive attitude when I get upset at myself, when I begin to feel the stress. When I get frustrated with myself, I look on the bright side so I feel better by what I'm trying to accomplish. Like I said, I know I feel like I'm carrying a lot more weight on my shoulders these days, but I try harder to do better.

The one thing that is difficult for students to understand, no matter what their age, is that fencing is a hard sport to learn. Period. It *is* hard. It takes time to work the process. The most important reason for doing the sport is the more intrinsic rewards of the challenge fencing provides and all the fun you have doing it, and not necessar-

Refereeing

ily for the external rewards, like results and medals. That has to be the focus. Jill says it's much more like learning a foreign language or playing a difficult instrument. You just have to stick with it. Fencing takes years to learn. Students are just impatient to get to the action.

Sometimes students don't give themselves enough margins to enjoy fencing and let the experience come, to let the experience happen on its own.

It's hard not to judge yourself too harshly. It comes with the territory. Jill says it's hard to accept the fact that you are going to lose and keep losing, and that you're going to lose more than you're going to win, but that's the challenge you have to accept for yourself. I know I've got to learn how to set realistic goals and find satisfaction in achieving them, even what seems like small goals.

Alex and Jill put a lot of emphasis on sportsmanship, on students showing respect and on being a good sport with their peers.

Kathryn and Renee

There are no professional fencers in the U.S. Fencers are not allowed to accept endorsements or win cash prizes. It is still deemed an amateur sport. If fencers do accept cash prizes, they will lose their ability to fence in the college and some high-level national tournaments.

Mariel Zagunis from Oregon is the first fencer in the world to hold four World Championship titles in one season: 2001 Cadet World Champion, 2001 Junior World Champion, 2001 Junior Team Champion and 2000 World Saber Team Champion.

Women's Foil was added to the events at the Olympic Games in 1924. Women's Epee was added in 1996. In 2004 the Olympic Games in Athens added Women's Saber in the official part of the Olympic program.

Until recently, women were permitted to compete only in foil, but now the USFA offers national competitions for women in epee and saber. Women's Epee was added to the World Championships in 1989. Things are looking up for women.

*"It is said so few saw his blade, but only
felt it when it found its mark"*

— Captain Kronos: 1974

PASSION

for the game...

I find nothing more pleasurable than competing and testing myself at local and national competitions with all I've learned at the Academy. Competitions are a good learning experience.

I haven't yet fenced internationally. That seems a long way off. I just have to make it through today, Saturday, because RIFAC is hosting a New England Division Championships tournament. And today I want to win a medal.

I go in as an individual for the events. The tournament is not considered a team event; it is all individual fencing. We train as a team, we're there supporting each

Alex goes over the day's events.

other as a team, we represent our club as a team, but the tournament is based on individual results.

Jill says the national rankings fencers get at national competitions are the real measure of a competitor. Finishing in the top 32 of a national tournament earn you points. Right now my goal is just to make it through the day and hopefully end up being a winner.

The national rankings go by point standings in certain age categories. My age group is Youth-14. I register under women's epee and my United States Fencing Association (USFA) classification is "U," or unclassified.

Initially the kids are **seeded** by their ratings and the year of that rating. You can improve your ratings at tournaments, but not lose them; ratings are only reduced if they are not renewed or improved on time.

Ratings for American fencers include U for unclassified, and E, D, C, B and A in order of achievement, with A being the highest classification and E being the lowest. A fencer will tell you, "I'm a CO5 in epee." This means she last earned or affirmed her C rating in the year 2005 for the epee.

Tournaments are divided by weapon. Since I'm an epee fencer, I will fence other epee fencers.

Sitting it out   *Preparing to unhook retractable cord.*

The tournament begins at three o'clock. Today the girls will fence. Sunday the boys will fence.

I enter the fencing club, rolling my large fencing bag behind me. I arrive early, about an hour or so before the competition begins. My parents go into the lounge area to wait for the tournament to begin.

The club is filled with excitement and anticipation and is jammed with fencers: foilists, epeeists and saberists, all potential medal winners. You can hear the clanging of blades and bell guards fill the room as competitors warm up in practice bouts. There's a long line at the counter as Jill checks the names of pre-registered fencers, so she knows who is here.

As I begin to warm up, Jill cries out, "Registration for foil is open." I have plenty of time to warm up before Jill calls the epee fencers next to register.

Alex says, "Foil fencers, please check your pool assignments and report to your strip immediately. Good luck to everybody."

I guess I'm real nervous, no matter how well-prepared I am. I really, really want to win a medal. I think my parents expect me to bring home a medal. Although I know the game is more important than the victory, and I know coaches don't measure success with medals, if I bring home a medal, it means to me that I have tried my hardest because I have the proof. I want to try my hardest. It helps me to know that all my hard work this year paid off. I'm intent on making it today, because I believe in myself and in my ability to overcome any obstacle that I will encounter.

Jill cries out, "If you are here to fence epee, please come over to the registration table." I go to the registration table and register for my tournament.

After I finish my warm-ups, I get suited up. My parents had bought all the fencing gear from the Academy.

Alex gives pool assignments.

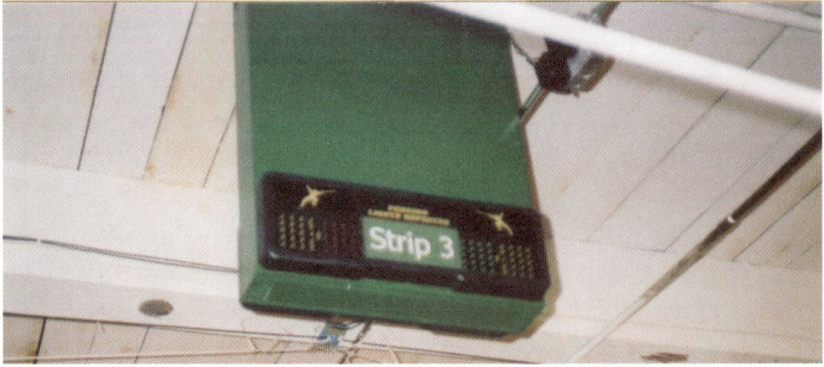

Scoring machines for Strip 1, Strip 2 and Strip 3

I'm already wearing my fencing shoes and white knickers. I use sneakers that are specifically designed for fencing.

First I put on a chest protector. All the girls have to use one. I then put on an underarm protector on my weapon-hand side to add a little more protection under my jacket, on the side that's likely to be hit.

Next, I put on my white fencing jacket. You actually step into a fencing jacket, with a strap that runs between the legs. The arm that you fence with is double-sleeved for added protection.

Before there was electric fencing, one way touches were recorded on the white surface of the jacket was with a wad of ink-soaked cotton on the tips of their weapons to mark the touch. Imagine all the horrible splotches on your uniform! I wouldn't like that.

The jacket also has a high collar that covers the neck. The first time I wore a jacket, I felt like I was stepping into a straight jacket, it was so confining, but I'm used to it now. I know I'm getting all the protection I need.

A **lame** is a metallic vest used in electric fencing and is put over your jacket to cover the valid target area. This makes it possible for a touch to register on the scoring machine. A lame is used only in foil and saber. Since I will be fencing in epee, I will not use a lame because my whole body is the target.

I fit on my mask down over my head. It has a protective bib, a heavy fabric below the mask which also protects my throat. The mask is wire-meshed and is somewhat adjustable. The first time I used a mask, it was hard to focus, and looking through the grille work made me slightly dizzy, but I'm used to it now.

The glove protects the weapon hand. You secure it with Velcro and wear it over the sleeve of your jacket. It provides a firm, nonslipping grip on your weapon. You must always fence with a glove. You do not use a glove on your unarmed hand.

A small spring-loaded tip is attached to the point of my epee and is connected to two wires inside the groove of the blade. I wear a body cord inside my jacket that plugs into the epee. The cord runs through the sleeve, out the back of my jacket, and connects to a retractable cord on a reel. The cord, which is connected to the scoring machine, plays out or takes up slack as I move back and forth on the strip.

The scoring machine is like a computer that has a timer and scoring lights. For epee, there are two scoring lights on the machine. When you hit your opponent in electric fencing, you depress the spring-loaded tip and the light goes on the scoring board, indicating you got the hit. A red light goes on for one fencer; a green light goes on for the opponent.

The epeeists fence practice bouts during the preliminary foil rounds. I fence with my friend, Lori.

After we have a few bouts we hear Jill call out, "Registration for epee closes in five minutes."

We know that the first round of our tournament is about to begin. Lori and I salute, shake hands, and go get a drink of water.

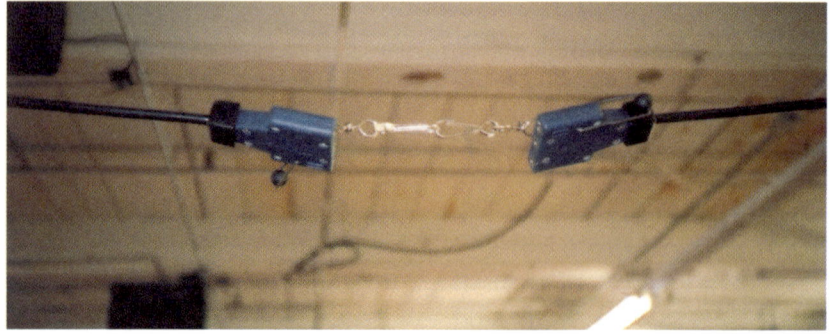

Retractable cord on a pulley to connect to a body cord

Registration for epeeists closes. The general list of epee fencers is posted. There are 25 of us, seeded 1 to 25 based on our ratings and the year of the rating. I check to see if everything concerning me on the list is correct.

There are five postings throughout the day for each weapon: the foil, the epee and the saber. There's an initial seeding posted of the participants at the competition, and then there's the list of pool assignments. The results of the pools are posted, followed by the direct elimination tableau. At the end, the final results are posted.

Alex, the meet manager, calls the epee referees together for a pow-wow. He goes over the day's proceedings with the referees, giving them remote controls for the score box at their strips, score sheets and clip boards with their pool assignments for the preliminary bouts.

He then calls out the names from the list of registered epee fencers and places them into pool assignments. I pick up my gear and go to my appropriate strip.

My referee goes to his assigned strip and he starts following the order of bouts listed on his score sheets. He tells me I will be up first, and then who will be next, or "on deck," as we say. He checks the score boxes, making sure they are properly set for the first bout, as my opponent and I hook up.

The fencers are distributed over five pools of five fencers each. Each pool has a strip, and they are separated so that all the skill levels are evenly spread out over each pool. Jill says that way you don't get all the top fencers in one pool and all the lower-level fencers in another pool.

In my pool I have five fencers, which means I will fence four bouts. We will fence five touch bouts and have three minutes of fencing time to do it. The first round is over when everybody in their pool has fenced everybody else in that pool.

DRESSING
to fence...

First Katie puts on her chest protector and underarm protector. She follows this by putting on her fencing jacket and plugging in her body cord (to electronically detect touches). Finally, she puts on her fencing gloves and her mask.

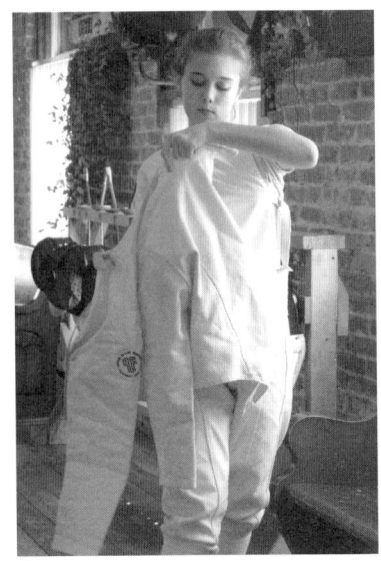

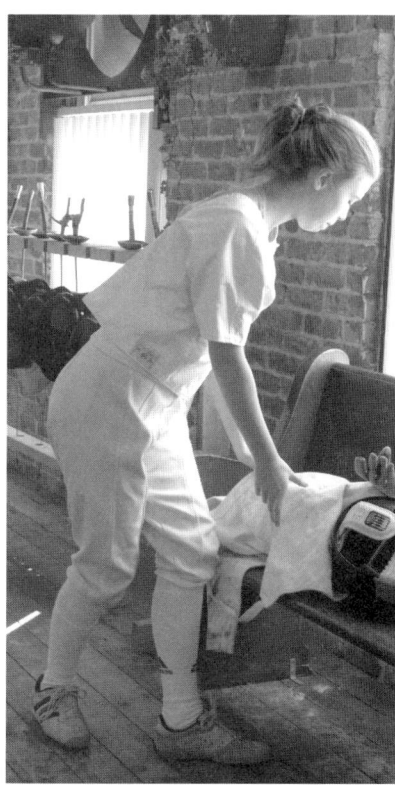

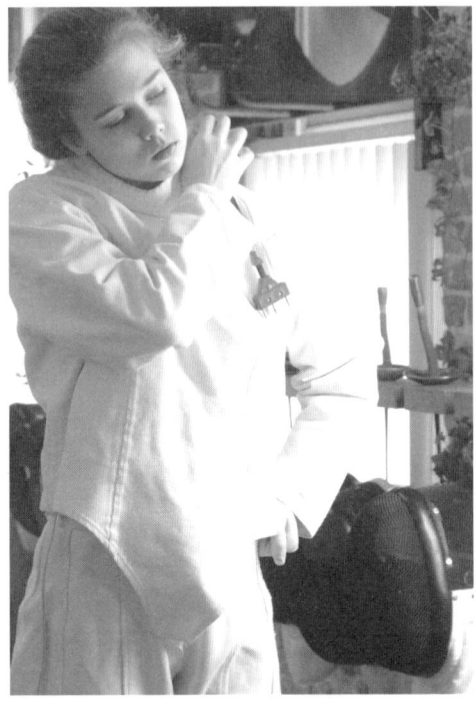

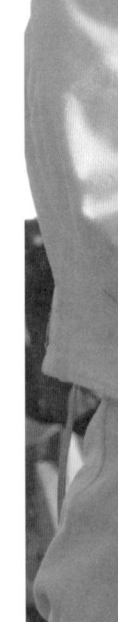

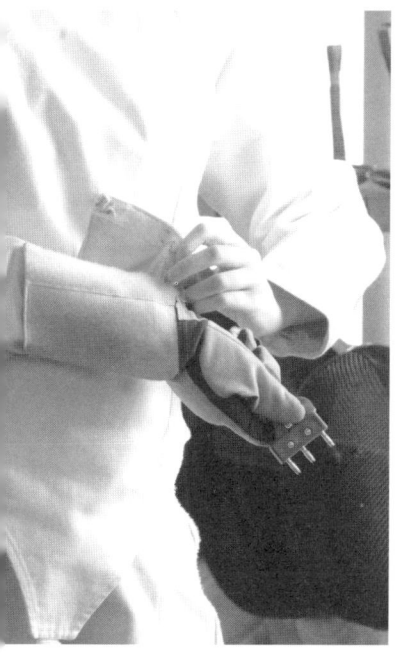

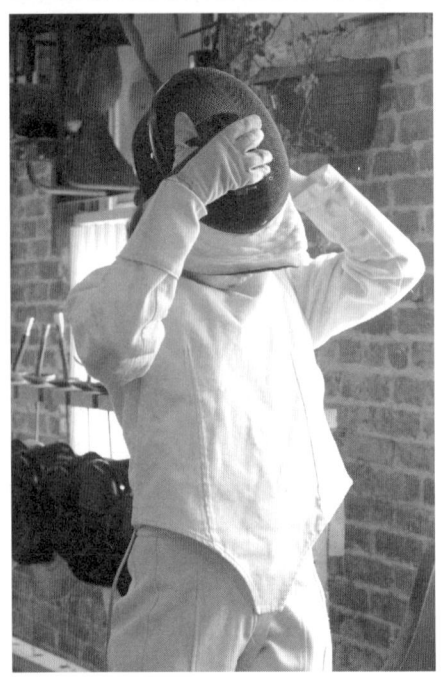

My pool bouts are fun and exciting. And quick, too. Three minutes go very fast, but usually someone gets five touches before the three minutes are up. The bouts give us a chance to get our juices flowing and prepare us for the direct elimination (or D.E.) bouts later on. The results of our pool will also determine the seeding after the pool and who will fence in the D.E.'s. I win three out of the four bouts in my pool.

When my pool is over, I look over the score sheet to make sure my scores are correct and then I sign the score sheet. All of the fencers will be placed on a **Direct Elimination Tableau,** or **D.E.,** based on their pool results, and all will receive a ranking to see where they stand. Since I won three of my bouts, I am hoping I am near the top of the list! The pools are a fight, but the D.E.'s are where the tournament really begins to take shape.

I quickly get something to eat and try to keep my mind focused. Nothing must distract me from what I want to achieve. I take a sip of water.

My parents give me encouraging words. I kiss my mom on the cheek. I know she is very proud of me. Dad gives me a hug.

The pool results in epee are posted. I check the seeding list. Then the tableau is posted with the strip assignments. I am ranked number eight out of 25. Since we will fence in a D.E. table of 32, the top seven fencers get a "bye," or automatically get to advance to the next round. Lucky fencers!

In Direct Elimination bouts I must score 15 points on my opponent before she scores that number on me. Each round of direct eliminations halves the number of competitors, as only the winners advance. I have to win to go on.

The time limit for direct elimination matches is nine minutes: three, three-minute periods with a one-minute break between each.

Jill explains that the D.E. tableau is arranged so that the top fencer will have to fence the bottom fencer and the second-to-the-top fencer would have to fence the second-to-the-bottom fencer, so by the time you get to the middle you are kind of fencing at even levels. This also prevents the top-seeded fencers from meeting each other until later in the tournament. Since I am ranked toward the top, I hope to win my first D.E. bout without too much hassle.

By the end of the tournament, the two fencers who make it to the last stage of the tableau will fight for first place. New ratings will be distributed to the top places. Medals are awarded to the top eight winners, with a gold, a silver and a bronze medal to the top three. I hope to make it to the final eight. I must win as many D.E.'s as I can!

The 25 fencers go to their respective strips to fence in their proper order. Bouts will go on at the same time.

I go to my strip and see my referee, Michael, looking at the list of fencers on his clipboard to see who is up first and who will immediately follow. He says, "Now fencing, it's Katie and Patty." I'm up first!

After we are hooked up, we hold our epees by their bell guards with the point up so the referee can check the springs in our tips with a cylinder-shaped instrument called a **weight,** to make sure they are working properly. Weapons sometimes fail weight tests because this main spring is too soft. Epee fencers just have to hit harder than foilists.

Michael also checks to see if we are hooked up correctly to the scoring machine.

He holds a remote control to clear the scoring machine to "0-0" and the three-minute time. Then he says, "Test guards, please."

Patty and I, each in turn, hit our points on the other fencer's guard to make sure that the score light will not

come on when the weapon is hit. It should only come on when we hit the opponent.

We stand behind the on-guard lines, salute each other, then salute the referee, and put on our masks.

The referee's hands are palm down.

"En garde. Ready." His palms go vertical.

"Fence!" His hands come together, palm against palm.

I face my opponent, my heart racing. Patty, who is ranked #13, immediately crouches down as if to spring at me like a cat. I wonder what her opening move will be. And how will I respond? Maybe I can provoke some reaction from her. I tap her bell guard to instigate a response. She immediately leaps off her leading foot, attempts to make a hit, but misses as she passes me at a run. I pull back just in time as she makes her move, swing around, and hit her in her back. I score!

"Halt!" Michael cries. "Touch arrives. The score is 1-0."

Patty made what is called a **fleche**. She looked very much like an arrow when she executed it. Epeeists seem to love making fleches.

It all comes down to strategy. The strategy is to win with the least number of moves. Just like a game of chess!

All the moves Jill and Alex taught me race through my mind, like notes in a rolodex. It's a nail-biting first period.

I think of actors and how they use their fears and anxiousness performing on stage to their advantage, using all that pent-up energy to "make it work" for them. Like I once did on the opening night of *A Christmas Carol*. But I know I mustn't be all worked up now. It's not good to be tense. I need to relax and remain calm and cool and focused because I have a lot of bouts ahead of me.

Patty and I continue to fence. Cautiously, at first, moving up and down the strip as one advances and the other retreats, gauging each other, determining what the other might do. The image of chess pieces moving on a chess board come to mind.

My opponent almost succeeds in driving me off the end of the strip. If she succeeded, the referee would stop the action, and I would lose a point to her. In the old days, to retreat behind this line during a duel labeled you a coward, and you would lose your honor. I try to prevent this from happening.

When Patty or I score a touch, the referee calls, "Halt!" and then indicates who is awarded the point. We are just at the beginning. He announces the score, "Katie, 3-1." I'm ahead!

We continue.

I extend my weapon arm and then explosively straighten my rear leg, launching my body forward towards Patty, landing on the heel of my front foot, decreasing the distance between us. This is called a **lunge.**

Patty immediately parries my attack, but doesn't follow through with a **riposte,** an immediate counteroffensive action. Instead, with blade against blade, I continue

putting my point forward, my blade remaining in the same line. I did not withdraw my weapon arm. I score a hit. This is called a **remise.** Yes! Now the score is 4-1.

Since epee fencers do not use right-of-way, we score a point simply by hitting our opponent first.

We continue. Patty and I both hit each other at the same time, both the red and green lights go on and we both receive a point, which is called a **double touch.**

My opponent is both quick and graceful. And very, very cunning. But I will outsmart her. I enjoy the challenge Patty provides, and my determination to score a point increases.

I see my parents watching me out of the corner of my eye. They have anxious expressions on their faces. I don't want to disappoint them. I know they plan to take me to dinner later to celebrate my "victory." I only hope they realize that I might not get a medal, although that is what I strongly desire.

My parents used to put too much pressure on me, just by watching every step of my training and constantly giving me advice. I know my parents feel pride in me, but unfortunately the pressure usually had the opposite effect. They kept demanding more from me, to win as many awards as I could. When that happens, forget it, I'm done. But now, they are starting to see how much I can accomplish if I'm left to my own devices and pace. I want my parents to remember that I chose fencing on my own, as my own expression of achievement, my own expression of self. It's a wonderful thing, too!

Alex and Jill have given me good strategies to stay focused on the bout, even though I see my parents nervously looking on.

The score now is 13-12 in my favor. This is really, really close. What a way to begin! Patty has nothing to

lose in this bout, everything goes, and that is exactly what Patty is trying to do.

Patty and I spend several minutes probing each other's defenses and maneuvering for distance before risking an attack. I might choose to stay on the defensive throughout the entire bout, but not always. I like to take well-calculated risks, too, when I know I have a good chance of scoring a point.

Patty attempts a lunge of her own, which I successfully parry. I immediately make a risposte. Yes! The score is now 14-12 and I am one touch away from winning my first D.E. bout.

During the break, Alex tells me it is necessary to analyze Patty's moves and develop a strategy to counter them to get the last touch. I think about the days when I had some free time to visit the Academy to observe the really experienced fencers' techniques and styles, to pick up pointers I didn't get in class. I like to think I have a style of my own.

I now visualize a well-timed counterattack that I feel confident I can make because I know Patty will be attacking me soon since time is running out.

With only a minute to spare, Patty launches her attack. Just as she is about to hit me, I duck and hit her first on her thigh. I win the bout, 15-12. It was too close for comfort! We salute each other and shake hands.

We both did a great job and thank each other for an exiting bout. I unhook myself from the reel and move to the side. I will have about ten minutes until I'm called up again.

I wonder how the other competitors are doing, and who I will be fencing in the later matches.

Now I fence Donna, who is ranked #9. She's also a U, or unclassified fencer. I need to beat her in order to get to the top eight. I enjoy fencing with her because she is a close friend. Sometimes it is hard knowing one of us must lose this bout.

She scores a touch right away. The referee cries out, "Halt!" His hand goes straight up on Donna's side. He stops the clock. "Score is 1-0." He presses a button on his remote control to advance the score on Donna's side.

Michael gets us into position again. "En garde. Ready. Fence!" He starts the clock with his remote control.

Donna immediately comes at me, and I immediately retreat, keeping my distance and keeping my cool.

Donna and I constantly move back and forth in a straight line within the confines of the strip, but when she corners me, I have to react quickly. I'm constantly thinking and planning and attacking. I like to focus. Focus makes me move forward. And I do. Now *she* is on the retreat.

The first three-minute period is over. The referee calls out, "Halt! That's the end of the first period. You have a one-minute break. The score is still just 1-0."

Alex consults with me again and gives me good instruction on how I should proceed in the bout, based on what has happened so far. He has been watching Donna closely and tells me how she is fencing and what I should do to outwit her.

Donna and I continue to fence, both of us scoring touches.The referee cries, "Halt! Double touch! The score is 2-1."

Time passes quickly and our scores climb.

Michael calls out, "This is the third and final three-minute period of fencing." The score is now 14-7 in my favor.

Again Alex gives me personal instruction during the second break of the bout. He reiterates that everybody has a different fighting style. That I must watch and learn the fighting style of my opponent to determine how to beat her. He repeats this idea to me many times because it is very important.

I salute my opponent and the referee.

You can almost feel the anticipation and excitement fall over the audience as we come 'on guard' in a semi-crouched position, our masks down and our weapons raised. My friends Melanie, Kristen, Mary, and Lisa are cheering me on. I get real support from my friends and other club members.

Michael uses both hands palm down for "en garde." Then he says, "Ready." His palms face us. "Fence!" He pushes his palms together.

Donna and I begin to implement well-practiced strategies, relying on hard-trained speed and deftness of feet.

Donna attempts an attack and I try to parry it, but she gets around my parry with a quick **disengage**, and I step back. It's been difficult getting out of her way because she's so fast, but I work on it.

I used to get real upset at myself when I couldn't disengage. I would just walk outside the Club and kind of let it roll off me, but I can't do that now. I work on trying not to get upset or angry at myself, and I try to maintain a positive attitude and do better next time around. I try to keep cool under the intense pressure. I do this by focusing on the bout and what I have to do to win.

Sometimes I will make a false attack, a **feint**, to probe and gauge the types of reactions and possible defenses I think Donna will make. Much of the fencing bout consists of preparation during which a fencer will determine her opponent's true intentions while feeding false information of her own.

Michael says we have twenty-three seconds remaining in the period.

Sometimes I don't put enough pressure on myself to achieve my goal when I need to put more on. You have to be energized to fight hard. It's a difficult balance.

Donna advances, I retreat. Donna stops and I lunge. She retreats again. I step up and lunge again. Donna parries, and I immediately evade her blade with a disengage and make a touch!

"Halt!" Michael puts up his right hand. I've made the last touch! "The score is 15-9."

I win and move to the next round. I have made it to the top eight!

I remove my mask, salute Donna, and shake her hand as we both congratulate each other on a job well done.

Now I will fence to get into the top four.

Michael clears the score and time on the scoring machine with his remote control, resetting the clock for the next bout. He gives the bout slip to me, and I take it up to Jill so she can record it on her computer.

Then I take a well-deserved drink of water. I worked hard during that bout!

I watch the next bout before I'm up again. It's a chance to cool down and reconnect with the event.

In the next match, Michelle is my opponent. She is ranked #17.

Michelle and I get into our "en garde" positions. The thought that this is the one bout that I *must* win sends my heart racing and I try to keep in control, focusing on the bout at hand.

But I know Michelle won't make it easy for me. She has as much to lose as I do.

After an exciting bout I won't soon forget, I win by one point, 15-14. I'm in the top four!

I wait for the other bout to finish. I wonder who I will fence with next. It's going to be Tina. Tina is ranked #5. She beats Rachel, 15-12.

The bout between Laura and Pam will go on at the same time as my bout.

Tina and I salute each other. We get into our "en garde" position and fence. But after a fierce battle with Tina, I lose the bout, 10-13, because the time ran out.

Pam loses to Laura, 15-12. Tina will move on to the next round against Laura, who is ranked #3. They are going for the gold.

I've lost against Tina, but it puts me in the bronze medal fence-off with Pam. Pam is ranked #7.

The referee says, "You need to check your scores and sign before you leave the strip."

Sometimes it is hard to congratulate my opponent when I just lost to her, but I'm a good loser. Tina and I hug each other.

Alex calls out, "The gold medal bout for epee is happening on Strip A." Everyone goes to watch it. It's Tina against Laura. I know that will be a tough one. The loser will get the silver medal.

In the first three-minute period between Pam and me, I execute a toe touch.

Jill cries out, "Oh! Nice touch!" It's nice to be recognized by your coaches!

A **toe touch** is a really neat move that requires a fencer to hit the toe of her opponent. It is really fun to do, but very hard to do because my opponent's feet are moving all the time. It's a move that I've worked hard on to master, and I did it! It was really sweet when I pulled that off. I savor the moment!

I told my parents, who have come to a tournament for the very first time, to focus on one fencer. It is difficult to follow the lightning speed of two fencers' actions. I know they are focusing on me. I hope they saw the toe touch I made.

I slide my blade along Pam's blade and hit her mask. The score machine buzzes and the lights come on. The referee cries, "Halt!" and we stop.

Pam gets me in my leg, then my arm. She likes to go for my limbs, it seems. She also likes to bounce a lot on her feet, which makes me a bit apprehensive.

I try to keep a safe distance from Pam, that is, out of range of her attacks. Then, either one of us will try to break this distance to gain an advantage for an attack.

Alex calls out, "Try something new, Katie, something new."

I try to score a touch by hitting Pam's shoulder with a quick flick of my blade. I know **flicks** are hard to do because I need to be able to depress the tip of my blade hard enough to score, but I go for it anyway because she just doesn't expect it and she's too late to deflect it. I slide my blade along hers, raise my arm, rising on my feet, and move close to her. I make a sudden and explosive flick on her wrist and score a touch. Unbelievable! I did it!

"Nice touch, Katie," Alex calls out. "Nice touch."

The score is now 13-9 in my favor.

Alex urges me on as we fence. "Let's go, Katie." The tension builds as we get to the final seconds of the bout. Pam keeps plugging away at me. She's an aggressive fencer. And she keeps bouncing!

I see my parents watching on the sidelines, cheering me on.

"Come on, Katie, this is yours!" they cry together.

I forget to breathe. Jill always reminded us to breathe. I must remember to breathe.

I get the final point and win the bout 15-12!

My parents leap up from their seats. My friends cheer my victory.

I pull off my mask and thrust my hands into the air in celebration of my moment of victory.

Tina beats Laura, 15-12. Time had run out and Laura wasn't able to make the touches to get ahead. Tina will get the gold.

Alex says, "All right, epeeists, we will immediately have the awards for the top eight finalists in women's epee."

The award ceremony begins.

Alex introduces his presenter, Jill, who really doesn't need an introduction at all because everyone knows her. She's a medal winner in her own right.

Alex says, "When I call your name, please come up."

I hear the names being called out, and I am so excited when it is my turn to stand in the row of the top eight finalists.

After announcing eighth through fourth place, Alex says, "Our bronze medalist in epee is Katie Walker."

I go up and get my medal. My mother is crying.

I shake hands with Alex, who congratulates me. Jill places the medal over my head, and I shake hands with her, then the other finalists.

Alex calls Laura, the silver medalist, and finally, "And our champion, our gold medalist, Tina Sterling."

Alex congratulates all of us. "Congratulations to our champion and all our finalists. The top seven fencers have qualified for the Summer Nationals."

Yes, I have made my goal! I won a medal today and qualified for the national championships!

As a fencer, I learn to incorporate the intellect of a chess player, the strength of a ballet dancer, the philosophy of a martial arts student and the cunning of a drama student. I have to have an acute sense of concentration to guide myself through several calculations to win. But nothing beats all the ceremony and tradition that are so much like the first noblemen who first practiced the art.

Fencing has profoundly affected my life. I respect the challenge that fencing innately provides, and I know something more about myself and what my limits are. I will forever be attuned to my physical abilities and the endurance fencing provides me. I'll be a better person. A good balanced person. RIFAC and fencing have taught me that!

"I know nothing of the sword; I need instruction"
– Scaramouche: 1952

GLOSSARY

1) ADVANCE: The fencer takes a step toward her opponent. She moves in the guard position; the front foot first, followed by the back foot.

2) ATTACK: The fencer takes an offensive action or series of actions toward her opponent by extending her sword arm and continuously threatening the valid target area of her opponent to score a point.

3) BOUT: An encounter between two fencers, at which a score is kept, either in a tournament or in practice, usually lasting five touches or three minutes, and in direct elimination, lasting 15 touches or nine minutes.

4) DISENGAGE: To make a circular motion with your blade that evades your opponent's parry. It moves the blade from engagement by passing under your opponent's blade.

5) DISTANCE: The space between you and your opponent that fencers maintain throughout a bout.

6) DRY: Fencing without electric scoring aids. Used during practice. A referee helps to keep score.

7) ENGAGEMENT: The first contact between the fencers' blades, often as a prelude to an attack.

8) EN GARDE (On Guard): The fencing position or stance that fencers assume before fencing commences.

9) EPEE: A fencing weapon with a large bell guard. Epee fencing has no right-of-way, and the whole body is the target.

10) FEINT: A false attack made by a fencer, with the intention of switching to another line of attack before the attack is completed to get a defensive reaction from the opposing fencer.

11) FENCING: The sport of fighting with swords.

12) FLECHE: Fleche literally means "arrow." An explosive attack in which the aggressor leaps off her leading foot, attempts to make a hit, and then passes her opponent at a run.

13) FLICK: A cut-like action that lands the point with a whip of the foible of the blade.

14) FOIL: A fencing weapon with a small bell guard used for practice. The foil has a limited target area: only the torso, front and back.

15) JUMP FORWARD: A fencer may gain ground by skipping forward and landing on both her feet at the same time, in the en garde position.

16) JUMP LUNGE: A fencer makes a lunge after completing a jump forward.

17) LAME: A vest worn over a jacket used to detect valid touches, only in foil or saber. Used in electric fencing.

18) LUNGE: An attack made by a fencer by pushing off from and extending her rear leg, launching herself at her opponent, and landing on her bent front leg, decreasing the distance between her weapon and her opponent's target area. You recover by returning to an en garde position after lunging.

19) PARRY: A deflecting action of an attack made by your opponent, in which a fencer blocks her opponent's blade.

20) PISTE: The linear strip on which the fencing bout is fought, approximately 2-meters wide and 14-meters long.

21) POINT: A valid touch made by hitting the target area of your opponent.

22) REDOUBLEMENT: A new action by an advancing fencer that follows an attack that she missed or was parried by her opponent. The attacker returns to her en garde position after her opponent avoids her attack by retreating.

23) REMISE: An immediate resumption of an attack that missed or was parried, without withdrawing the arm.

24) RETREAT: Taking a backward step in the en garde position when your opponent advances toward you. You move the back foot first, followed by the front foot.

25) RIGHT-OF-WAY: The governing rule for awarding the point to the fencer who attacks first in the event of a double touch. Used only in foil and saber.

26) RIPOSTE: A defender's offensive action made immediately after successfully parrying her

opponent's attack.

27) SABER: A fencing weapon used with cutting or thrusting actions. Saber fencing includes right-of-way and has a limited target area: the body from the waist up. You may score with the edge of the saber.

28) SALUTE: A fencer, with her weapon, makes a respectful acknowledgement of her opponent and referee at the start and end of a bout.

29) TARGET (AREA): The area on the fencer's body where a score is made by a touch. In foil, the target area includes the torso only, the front, back and sides of your opponent's body. In epee, the target area includes the whole body, from head to toe, including your opponent's arms, hands and feet. In saber, the target area includes everything from the waist up, including the head.

30) TEMPO: The general pace of a combination action between opponents.

31) TOUCH: A hit on a valid target area with the tip or edge of your weapon on your opponent. A touch stops the fencing action.

For an extended list of fencing terms, refer to the glossary at **www.fencing.net**.

for more information

Organizations

United States Fencing Association (USFA)
One Olympic Plaza
Colorado Springs, CO 80909-5774
(719) 866-4511
www.info@usfencing.org

International Fencing Federation (F.I.E.)
Maison Du Sport International
Avenue de Rhondorie 54
CH--1007
Lausaunne, Suisse
41 21 320 31 15
www.fie.ch

U.S. Olympic Team
U.S. Olympic Training Center
Colorado Springs National Headquarters
One Olympic Plaza
Colorado Springs, CO 80909-5774
(719) 623-5551

Rhode Island Fencing Academy and Club (RIFAC)
16 Cutler Street, Third Floor
Warren, RI 02885
(401) 245-7902
www.rifac.com

Magazines and Newsletters

Fencer's Quarterly
848 S. Kimbrough
Springfield, MO 65806
(417) 866-4370
Contact: Justin E. Evangelista, Managing Editor

Hammerterz Forum (Quarterly)
P.O. Box 13448
Baltimore, MD 21203

Cut and Thrust (Journal)
Ronin M/A Publications
34-3 Shunpike Road
Dept. 162
Cromwell, CT 06416

American Fencing (a quarterly newsletter)
Cindy Bent Findley, Editor and U.S. Fencing
Media Coordinator
(614) 746-6773
www.americanfencingmagazine.com
www.usfencingmediaearthlink.net

The Sword: British Fencing
1 Baron's Gate
33 Rothschild Road
London, W4 5HT England
www.britishfencing.com

Academy of Arms: Online Quarterly
www.clarityconnect.com

www.guardup.com (online store)
(781) 270-4800

about the author

Carlos Velez III is the writer, producer and director of an original live mystery/suspense series, "Night Voices, Radio Theatre for the New Age Mind," on Cape Cod. "Night Voices" revives and celebrates the art of live radio suspense stories of the 1930s, 40s, and 50s. He has been involved in all aspects of theater for seventeen years and received ACTE's 1991-1992 Evelyn Lawson Award for outstanding achievement in lighting and technical design for Tennessee Williams' *Cat on the Hot Tin Roof*, and received the Midwest Radio Theatre Workshop's 1998 Grand Prize for the radio script, *The Dark Screen*, a tribute to Alfred Hitchcock and Cornell Woolrich. He has also directed the Falmouth Theater Guild's production of *The Hound of the Baskervilles* and recently directed his one-act suspense play, "The Long Wait," at the Barnstable Comedy Club on Cape Cod. He has written several two-act plays and mystery novellas and has recently completed a detective murder mystery novel about Hollywood in the 1930s. He is currently working on a nonfiction book for young adults entitled *How To Write, Produce and Direct Live Audio Theater*.